looking back at ...

THE 1966 WORLD CUP

Published by Cognitive Books Limited,
115 New Road, Croxley Green WD3 3EN. United Kingdom
Published by Cognitive Books, 2024

Text © Matt Singleton, 2024
Illustrations © Samuel Larn, 2024
Original photograph of England's victory (cover and pages 26, 78 and 80) © Trinity Mirror / Mirrorpix / Alamy Stock Photo
Icons pages 65-72: © Oliviart (Newspaper), GRAYSCVLE (Film), kavya (TV), Barudak Lier (Music) all /AdobeStock

ISBN: 978-1-7384591-1-7

This book has primarily been developed and published for those living with dementia and their loved ones.
This is not intended to be an official history of the 1966 World Cup. However, every attempt has been made to
research the topic thoroughly and any inaccuracies are unintentional.

The phrase 'They think it's all over … it is now!' used in the book is from the famous BBC coverage of the
1966 World Cup Final by Kenneth Wolstenholme and is used under the quotation exception in the Copyright,
Designs and Patents Act 1988.

We are committed to working with print partners who prioritise environmental and social responsibility.
Printed and bound in Latvia by PNB Print.

www.cognitivebooks.co.uk

looking back at ...

THE 1966 WORLD CUP

Written by Matt Singleton

Illustrations by Samuel Larn

COGNITIVE
BOOKS.

Download the free audio version of this book – read by iconic football commentator, Clive Tyldesley – at cognitivebooks.co.uk/download or by scanning the QR code.

If you're the supporter (e.g. a carer or a loved one) of the person reading this book, you can enjoy it too! There are some useful hints and tips for you on pages 76 and 77 of this Cognitive Book to make sure everyone gets the most out of it.

Become a Cognitive Bookworm at cognitivebooks.co.uk

This book has been created in collaboration with Alzheimer's Society. 5% of the publisher's proceeds from the sale of this Cognitive Book will be paid to the charity. The aim of Cognitive Books is to increase this contribution over time. Alzheimer's Society is the FA's official charity partner (2021-2024). The two organisations work together to use the power of football to raise awareness of dementia and break down the barriers to accessing support.

You can find lots of useful information to support people living with dementia at alzheimers.org.uk

For my Dad, Brian.
Thank you for all our footballing memories.
With love from, Matt x

With special thanks to the team at Alzheimer's Society, especially
Graeme and Sarah, the team at the FA, Clive, Sam, Sarah,
Nicky, Nicola, Gill, Adelina, my colleagues at Swiss Re and – as always –
Colleen, Claire, William, Ben and (as ever) Smidge The Cat.

Matt Singleton, 2024

Contents

Foreword   7

The story of the 1966 World Cup   9

Exercises   45

    Just for fun – it's quiz time   46

    Some more quiz questions   51

    Did we know?   54

    Let's chat   56

    England's route to World Cup glory   60

    The story of the 1965-66 football season   62

    What happened in the United Kingdom in 1966?   65

    Quiz answers   73

Supporters' guide   76

Foreword by Sir Geoff Hurst

Dear Reader,

1966 holds a special place in my heart. Scoring a hat-trick in a World Cup final is a dream for so many children when they're growing up. To see that dream become a reality … well, I still find it hard to believe it happened to me.

Lots of people have memories to share of that perfect World Cup summer and it's a privilege to hear them. My memories are all about my teammates. After the final whistle, Bobby Charlton said to his brother, Jack, that our lives will never be the same. He was absolutely right!

I've lost too many of those teammates, including dear Bobby and Jack, to this dreadful condition, dementia. But I'm only too aware that there are moments of joy during someone's dementia journey. It would be fantastic if this book brings several of those moments and invokes wonderful memories for many readers.

I hope you enjoy this book, all about the most amazing period in men's English football history (so far), as much as I do!

Sir Geoff Hurst, June 2024

Before the World Cup

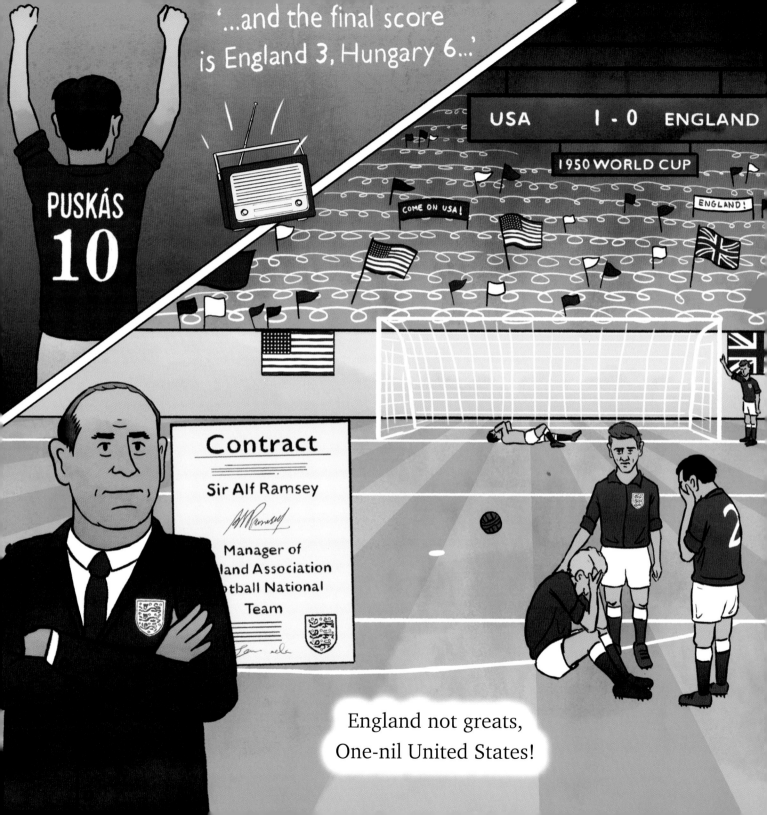

1950 to 1963: A time of disappointment

Before they were World Champions, they assumed they were the best,
But England failed, 1950, their first true World Cup test.
Winterbottom's boys turned out, in Brazil, to be not greats,
Humility did beckon them, one-nil United States.
Three years later, worse still yet, a trouncing came to pass,
Wembley, six-three, Hungary, a right pain in Puskás!
Forward on to '63, Sir Alf (just 'Alf' back then),
Handed reigns of national team: two halves; eleven men.

There might be no more blunders,
For Ramsey's 'Wingless Wonders'!

1963 to 1966: The World Cup build-up

Ramsey, now, the sole boss, no dark backroom committee,
Free to pick from anywhere: United, Town or City.
In 1963 Alf says, in perfect, clipped, Queen's diction,
'England will win the next World Cup!' – a rather bold prediction.
Winning against Spain suggests there might be no more blunders,
A four-three-three formation, that the press names 'Wingless Wonders'.
The trophy shown in London, is stolen by some wally,
But soon retrieved by Pickles, a hero little collie!

Time passes like a supernova,
It really melts the heart,
Just when 'they think that it's all over',
It's just about to start.

The tournament

The fans observe the scene,
A speech from our young Queen!

11 July 1966: The World Cup kicks off

Rivals gather at Wembley, a feast of anticipations,

From faves Brazil to North Korea, it's sixteen footballing nations.

The ceremony opens, and the fans observe the scene,

The crowds, the pomp, the pageantry, a speech from our young Queen.

Our TV sets were black and white, but in colour we can now recall,

A spectacle so vivid, which includes the orange match ball.

Lonnie Donegan did sing, a record oh so silly,

About the contest's mascot: that lion, World Cup Willie!

The group stage:

England vs Uruguay (11 July 1966); England vs Mexico (16 July 1966); England vs France (20 July 1966)

The opener with Uruguay, disappoints: nil-nil,
To a film set England go, meet Bond (Licence to Kill).
Against Mexico a win is gained, it's two-nil on the cards,
Bobby Charlton's screamer hit from almost thirty yards.
Another two-nil, over France, with this time a debacle,
Both the goals to Roger Hunt, but there's Nobby's dirty 'tackle'!
Pelé's kicked and Italy out; Spain back home they flew,
England quarters, not Brazil, with North Korea through!

SEMI - FINAL   WEMBLEY 1966

ENGLAND   2 - 1   PORTUGAL

Bobby Charlton 31', 79'   Eusebio 83' (Pen)

A marking job for Nobby,
Two goals for Charlton (Bobby)!

The quarter- and semi-finals:

England vs Argentina (23 July 1966); England vs Portugal (26 July 1966)

The Argentina game's remembered for bringing out the worst,
The hair pulling, the fouls, yet not the goal by Geoffrey Hurst.
'Animals!' Alf Ramsey says, does not recant or yield,
Rattín's sent off from the match, but refuses to leave the field!

Portugal's Eusébio's marked out the game by Nobby,
And we march onto the final; two goals for Charlton (Bobby)!
Last few minutes, it's two-one when Eusebio succeeds,
A penalty, and it's the first goal England concedes.

Time passes like a supernova,
It seems to nearly whizz,
Just when 'they think that it's all over',
It never really is.

ENGLAND 2 GERMANY W. 2
After 90 Minutes
ENGLAND!
1-0
HALLER
8
OORE
6
HURST
10
DEUTSCHLAND
1-1
2-1
HUNT
21
WEBER
6
It seems like we will win it,
Till Weber scores last minute!
2-2!

The final – the first ninety minutes:

England vs West Germany (30 July 1966)

Over ninety thousand march to Wembley's Twin Towers,
To watch us meet the Seelers, and the Beckenbauers.
Twelve minutes counted in, and confidence does shake,
It's Haller, one-nil Germany, Ray Wilson's brief mistake.
A free kick is soon given, and Moore takes quick control,
Lobs the ball to teammate Hurst, an equalising goal!
Martin Peters bangs one in, it seems like we will win it,
Until the Germans scramble, and Weber scores last minute!

Moore's pass (oh so slick),
Finds Hurst for his hat-trick!

The final – extra time:

England vs West Germany (30 July 1966)

West Germany are seated, Alf Ramsey's got things planned,
'Show we're not defeated!' he makes his players stand.
Our manager he motivates, encourages his men,
'You've beaten them once before, now go beat them again!'
The game swings one way, then the next, inspiration comes divine,
The linesman rules that Geoff Hurst's shot did really cross the line.
The controversy is soon over, when Moore's pass (oh so slick),
Finds Hurst running through again: four-two (and hat-trick)!

Time passes like a supernova,
We remember with a wow,
Just when 'they think that it's all over',
Geoff's goal says, 'it is now!'

Nobby's toothless grin,
A dance for England's win!

After the match

Moore receives the trophy from the utmost noblesse,
Elizabeth The Second, in her yellow hat and dress.
He's soon on teammates' shoulders, to honour our great win,
Nobby Stiles dances a jig with wide and toothless grin!
Little did we realise, it would not happen again,
Not in Euros or World Cup (well, at least not for the men)!
But we hold dear these memories, relive them every day,
When Alf Ramsey, and his boys, lift high the Jules Rimet.

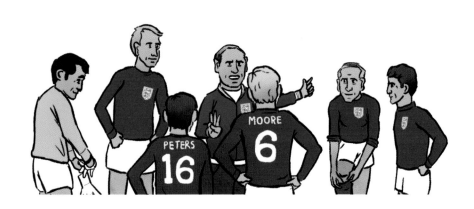

The manager and the players

Our expert boss with visions,
Wins top three league divisions!

The manager:

Sir Alfred 'Alf' Ramsey (1920-1999)

An Essex boy, not scholarly, a wartime quartermaster,
Alf defended land and pitch, great passer (could be faster).
Southampton's Saints and England, to him success is vital,
Onto Spurs, and soon Alf wins, a coveted league title.
At Ipswich Town, the boss's job, with expert forward visions,
England call soon after he wins top three league divisions.
A quiet man, keeps self to self, no fast cars, parties, boozing,
A focus deep on tactics, though, and strong hatred of losing.

Liverpool's man up front,
It's our champ, Roger Hunt!

Key men from our team:

George Cohen (1939-2022), **Ray Wilson** (1934-2018),
John 'Jack' Charlton (1935-2020), **Norbert 'Nobby' Stiles** (1942-2020),
Alan Ball (1945-2007), **Martin Peters** (1943-2019), **Roger Hunt** (1938-2021)

Players who played in the tournament but didn't play in the final:
Ian Callaghan (1942-), **John Connelly** (1938-2012), **Terry Paine** (1939-)

Cohen, Wilson, Jack Charlton, just great with Bobby Moore,
Fulham, Everton and Leeds: our solid, backline four.
Young Alan Ball of Blackpool, red hair and so unyielding,
With Nobby Stiles and Martin Peters, experts in midfielding!
It's Liverpool's great striker, controlling things up front,
Scores three World Cup vital goals – it's our champ, Roger Hunt.
Paine, Connelly and Callaghan: we really hope you've seen 'em,
In '66 they only make three appearances between them!

Rank	Player	Goals	Apps
1	Jimmy Greaves	357	516
2	Steve Bloomer	314	535
3	Dixie Dean	310	362
4	Gordon Hodgson	288	455
5	Alan Shearer	283	559
6	Charlie Buchan	258	481
7	David Jack	257	476
8	Nat Lofthouse	255	452
9	Joe Bradford	248	410
10	Hughie Gallacher	246	355
11	Joe Smith	243	416
12	George Brown	240	366

Our 'Greavsie' gets it right,
Most goals in the top flight!

The one who missed out:

James 'Jimmy' Greaves (1940-2021)

Jim is left out from the final, injury takes its toll,
A striker quite extraordinary, he always bags a goal!
From Chelsea, Milan to Tottenham, our 'Greavsie' gets it right,
And now his record's unsurpassed: most goals in the top flight.
He scores on every debut, for country and each club,
When he's not on the football field, you'd find him down the pub!
Later he's teetotal, shows courage and restraint,
Then forms a TV partnership with the Scotsman known as 'Saint'.

Our rock right at the back,
Could build the next attack!

The captain:

Robert 'Bobby' Moore (1941-1993)

The blonde and smiling number six, our rock right at the back,
Bobby Moore could win the ball, then build the next attack.
Our leader and our captain, he set the game's benchmark,
Remembered oh so fondly, at West Ham's Upton Park.
Not fast, but times things perfectly, impossible to beat,
That tackle on Jairzinho in Mexico's harsh heat!
This winner holds all the magic, we watch with bated breath,
Heartbreak at an end so tragic: a far too early death.

We must all give him thanks,
A hero: Gordon Banks!

The goalkeeper:

Gordon Banks (1937-2019)

From his humble beginnings, this gentle Yorkshire bloke,

Plies his trade at Chesterfield, Leicester City, Stoke.

Remembered most for that great save, in '70 World Cup melee,

Diving down to his right post, a strong header from Pelé!

When driving his Ford Consul, his steering goes awry,

It costs him his career; loses sight in his right eye.

Our yellow-shirted goalkeeper, we must all give him thanks,

For saving us from those defeats, a hero: Gordon Banks.

The virtuoso:

Sir Robert 'Bobby' Charlton (1937-2023)

Admired from Northumberland, right down south to Dover,
The power shot, that graceful glide, the wind blows his comb-over!
Bobby was a Busby Babe, a master and a great,
Survives the Munich air disaster, 1958.
An experience that shapes him, a kind man to his core,
Forms a winning trio, with Best and Denis Law.
Three of Man United's greats, there are no fine men sleeker,
He finally lifts the Euro Cup, 'gainst Eusébio's Benfica.

Attacking man with glamour,
A banging-goals-in Hammer!

The goal machine:

Sir Geoffrey 'Geoff' Hurst (1941-)

Many people aren't aware, our Geoff played first-class cricket,
Essex, one appearance: one catch, no runs, no wicket!
A football man, above all else, plays with grace and glamour,
Switched to attack, from defence, a banging-goals-in Hammer.
Relied upon by country, goal-scoring instincts primal,
Helps his club to victory, in '64's Cup Final.
Becomes a 'Sir' in '98, renowned in true propriety,
Now charity work, Ambassador, to Alzheimer's Society!

Time passes like a supernova,
All those chances taken,
Just when 'they think that it's all over',
Our hope can reawaken.

Exercises

Just for fun – it's quiz time!

These questions are from the story and all the answers can be found in the book! You get one mark for each with a total of fifteen points to get. The answers are on page 73.

1950-1963: A time of disappointment (page 11):

What nationality was Ferenc Puskás, who played a major role – including scoring two goals – in the 6-3 defeat of England at Wembley in 1953?
   a.   Hungarian
   b.   Czechoslovakian
   c.   Scottish

1963-1966: The World Cup build-up (page 13):

What was the name of the collie dog who found the Jules Rimet World Cup trophy after it was stolen shortly before the tournament kicked off?
   a.   Tickles
   b.   Mr Micklesford
   c.   Pickles

The World Cup kicks off (page 17):

What was the name of the lion mascot – and the name of the song by Lonnie Donegan – used to promote the 1966 World Cup in England?
  a.   World Cup Willie
  b.   Eric of England
  c.   Jules Rimmer

The group stage (page 19):

Which surprise team from Asia qualified for the quarter-finals – when Italy, Spain and Brazil didn't?
  a.   India
  b.   Japan
  c.   North Korea

The quarter- and semi-finals (page 21):

Who scored Portugal's only goal in the semi-final from the penalty spot – too late to prevent England's victory?
  a.   Pinto José Augusto
  b.   Eusébio
  c.   Mário Coluna

The final – the first ninety minutes (page 23):

Other than Geoff Hurst, who scored for England in the 1966 World Cup final against West Germany at Wembley?

a. Bobby Moore
b. Martin Peters
c. Roger Hunt

The final – extra time (page 25):

What did Alf Ramsey tell his team to do during the break before extra time to show their opponents that England's players still had energy?

a. Drink lots of water
b. Sing 'World Cup Willie'
c. Stand up

After the match (page 27):

Which toothless player danced a jig around the field after England's victory?

a. Nobby Stiles
b. George Cohen
c. Alan Ball

The manager: Sir Alfred 'Alf' Ramsey (1920-1999) (page 31):

With which football club did Alf Ramsey win the Football League Third Division (South), Second Division and First Division as a manager?
- a. Southampton
- b. Ipswich Town
- c. Coventry City

Key men from our team (page 33):

Which Liverpool striker played up front for England in the 1966 World Cup, scoring three vital goals during the tournament?
- a. Roger Hunt
- b. Bobby Moore
- c. Alan Ball

The one who missed out: James 'Jimmy' Greaves (1940-2021) (page 35):

Which Italian club did Jimmy Greaves play for during his career?
- a. AC Milan
- b. Sampdoria
- c. Parma

The captain: Robert 'Bobby' Moore (1941-1993) (page 37):

What number shirt did Bobby Moore wear for England and West Ham United?
- a. 33
- b. 6
- c. 11

The goalkeeper: Gordon Banks (1937-2019) (page 39):

In which World Cup did Gordon Banks make his amazing save, often called 'The Greatest Ever Save', from Pelé's header during the England game against Brazil?

  a.   Sweden, 1958

  b.   Mexico, 1970

  c.   Argentina, 1978

The virtuoso: Sir Robert 'Bobby' Charlton (1937-2023) (page 41):

Which Portuguese side did Manchester United beat to win the 1968 European Cup final – a game in which Bobby Charlton scored two goals?

  a.   Estrela Amadora

  b.   Braga

  c.   Benfica

The goal machine: Sir Geoffrey 'Geoff' Hurst (1941-) (page 43)

For which county did Sir Geoff Hurst play one game of first-class cricket?

  a.   Essex

  b.   Yorkshire

  c.   Glamorgan

Some more ...

Here are some questions where the answers aren't in the book!
Each question is worth one point (except the last, which is worth six).
There is a total of fifteen points to get. The answers are on page 75.

1. Which player won the 1966 World Cup Ballon d'Or (Golden Ball), awarded to the tournament's most outstanding player?
   a.   Bobby Charlton (England)
   b.   Pelé (Brazil)
   c.   Denis Law (Scotland)

2. Which team finished third in the tournament, after beating the USSR (Soviet Union) in the third place play-off, 2-1 at Wembley?
   a.   North Korea
   b.   Bulgaria
   c.   Portugal

3. From which country was the linesman, Tofiq Bahramov, who insisted that England's controversial third goal crossed the line in the final?
   a.   England
   b.   USSR (Soviet Union)
   c.   West Germany

4. Who was the top scorer – also known as the Golden Boot winner – during the 1966 World Cup tournament, with nine goals to his name?
  a.   Pak Seung-zing (North Korea)
  b.   Eusébio (Portugal)
  c.   René-Pierre Quentin (Switzerland)

5. Other than West Ham United, for which of the following football clubs did Bobby Moore play during his professional career?
  a.   Fulham
  b.   Bristol City
  c.   Queen of the South

6. How many international goals did Bobby Charlton score for England's first team – a record that stood from his last goal for England in May 1970, until Wayne Rooney beat it in September 2015?
  a.   12
  b.   134
  c.   49

7. Which BBC TV commentator said the immortal lines, 'Some people are on the pitch … they think it's all over … it is now!' as Geoff Hurst scored the final goal to complete the 4-2 victory for England in extra time?
  a.   Kenneth Wolstenhulme
  b.   Kenny Rogers
  c.   Ken Dodd

8. Who was the captain of the West Germany team in the 1966 World Cup final?

  a.   Uwe Seeler

  b.   Gottfried Dienst

  c.   Helmut Kohl

9. Jack Charlton went from World Cup glory to have a successful managerial career – but which national football side did he lead to qualification in the 1990 and 1994 World Cups, reaching the quarter finals in 1990 and the round of 16 in 1994?

  a.   Ghana

  b.   Luxembourg

  c.   Republic of Ireland

10. The following stadiums were used to host matches in the tournament. Can you name which clubs played their home games there in 1966? There are six to get:

Roker Park ....

Old Trafford ....

Hillsborough ....

Ayresome Park ....

Villa Park ....

Goodison Park ....

Did we know?

Some facts about the story of the 1966 World Cup that aren't so well known!

? *Did we know* that England lost 1-0 to the USA on 29 June 1950 at the World Cup in Brazil? This was regarded as a low point for English football. Three years later, on 25 November 1953, England were defeated 6-3 by Puskás' Hungary in what was referred to as the 'match of the century'. Who was England's right-back in both these games? None other than Alf Ramsey!

? *Did we know* that prior to Alf Ramsey taking over the team, Walter Winterbottom was England manager from 1946 to 1962? Winterbottom had no football management experience before being appointed and had made just twenty-six senior appearances as a Manchester United player! In those days, the England team was selected by a committee. Alf Ramsey was the first manager to have control over team selection.

? *Did we know* that Geoff Hurst was originally a left half, but Ron Greenwood – his manager at West Ham – was more impressed with his goalscoring skills than his other capabilities? It was Greenwood who switched Hurst to his more familiar role as striker.

? *Did we know* that when Gordon Banks made that great save from Pelé in the 1970 World Cup, the Brazilian great was so confident he had scored that he shouted, 'Goal!' as the ball left his head at lightning speed? He could not believe Banks managed to push the ball over the cross bar! Apparently, there was an on-field exchange between three great players soon after the event:

> *Pelé: I thought that was a goal.*
> *Banks: You and me both!*
> *Bobby Moore (a renowned joker): You're getting old, Banksy, you used to hold onto them!*

? *Did we know* that when going to receive the World Cup (Jules Rimet) trophy from Queen Elizabeth II, Bobby Moore noticed that Her Majesty was wearing white gloves? To spare her having to shake his sweaty, dirty hands, he wiped them on the velvet covering of Wembley's Royal Box!

Let's chat

Here are some conversation topics for you to talk about – or even just think about. There's also some space to write notes if needed.

- Which is your favourite football club, if you have one? What stories are there about the club – perhaps famous matches, some of the players or the other events associated with that team? If you don't have a favourite team, pick a club that's well known to you.

- Who is your all-time favourite English football player? What makes you say that? What about players from other countries? Who do you most admire, and why?

- Thinking about football from your childhood, what has changed about the game since then?

- Did you ever play football? If yes, what position did you prefer? What team(s) did you play for, if any? What were you like as a footballer? Who else did you play with?

- What other major events can you think of from the 1960s? Perhaps from the music world, television, the news or even your own, or your family and friends', lives from that time? There are some reminders on later pages (pages 65 to 72) which may prompt your thoughts!

Which is your favourite football club, if you have one? What stories are there about the club – perhaps famous matches, some of the players or the other events associated with that team? If you don't have a favourite team, pick a club that's well known to you.

Who is your all-time favourite English football player? What makes you say that? What about players from other countries? Who do you most admire, and why?

....

....

....

....

....

....

Thinking about football from your childhood, what has changed about the game since then?

....

....

....

....

....

Did you ever play football? If yes, what position did you prefer? What team(s) did you play for, if any? What were you like as a footballer? Who else did you play with?

....

....

....

....

....

What other major events can you think of from the 1960s? Perhaps from the music world, television, the news or even your own, or your family and friends', lives from that time? There are some reminders on later pages (pages 65 to 72) which may prompt your thoughts!

....

....

....

....

England's route to World Cup glory

11 July 1966
England 0-0 Uruguay
Wembley Stadium, attendance: 87,148

 England 2-0 Mexico
16 July 1966

B. Charlton (37 mins)
Hunt (75 mins)
Wembley Stadium, attendance: 92,570

20 July 1966
  England 2-0 France
Hunt (38, 75 mins)
Wembley Stadium, attendance: 98,270

GROUP 1 FINAL TABLE

	TEAM	PLAYED	WON	DRAWN	LOST	GOAL RATIO	POINTS
1	England (qualify for knockout stage)	3	2	1	0	–	5
2	Uruguay (qualify for knockout stage)	3	1	2	0	2.00	4
3	Mexico	3	0	2	1	0.33	2
4	France	3	0	1	2	0.40	1

QUARTER-FINAL

23 July 1966

 England 1-0 Argentina

Hurst
(77 mins)

Wembley Stadium, attendance: 90,584

SEMI-FINAL

26 July 1966

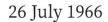 **England 2-1 Portugal**

| **B. Charlton** | **Eusébio** |
| (30, 80 mins) | (82 mins, penalty) |

Wembley Stadium, attendance: 94,493

FINAL

30 July 1966

 England 4-2 West Germany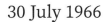
(After extra time)

Hurst	**Haller**
(18, 101, 120 mins),	(12 mins)
Peters	**Weber**
(78 mins),	(89 mins)

Wembley Stadium, attendance: 96,924

The story of 1965-66 football season

The Football League in 1966

First division: 1965 to 66 end of season table

	TEAM	PLAYED	WON	DRAWN	LOST	GOAL AVERAGE	POINTS
1	Liverpool (Champions)	42	26	9	7	2.32	61
2	Leeds United	42	23	9	10	2.08	55
3	Burnley	42	24	7	11	1.68	55
	Relegated to Division 2						
21	Northampton Town	42	10	13	19	0.60	33
22	Blackburn Rovers	42	8	4	30	0.65	20

Top goal scorers: Roger Hunt (Liverpool), Willie Irvine (Burnley) – 29 league goals each in the season.

Second division: 1965 to 66 end of season table

	TEAM	PLAYED	WON	DRAWN	LOST	GOAL AVERAGE	POINTS
	Promoted						
1	Manchester City (Champions)	42	22	15	5	1.73	59
2	Southampton	42	22	10	10	1.52	54
	Relegated to Division 3						
21	Middlesbrough	42	10	13	19	0.67	33
22	Leyton Orient	42	5	13	24	0.48	23

Top goal scorer: Martin Chivers (Southampton) – 30 league goals in the season.

Third division: 1965 to 66 end of season table

	TEAM	PLAYED	WON	DRAWN	LOST	GOAL AVERAGE	POINTS
	Promoted						
1	Hull City (Champions)	46	31	7	8	1.76	69
2	Millwall	46	27	11	8	1.77	65
	Relegated to Division 4						
21	Southend United	46	16	4	26	0.65	36
22	Exeter City	46	12	11	23	0.67	35
23	Brentford	46	10	12	24	0.70	32
24	York City	46	9	9	28	0.50	27

Top goal scorer: Les Allen (Queens Park Rangers) – 30 league goals in the season.

Fourth division: 1965 to 66 end of season table

	TEAM	PLAYED	WON	DRAWN	LOST	GOAL AVERAGE	POINTS
	Promoted						
1	Doncaster Rovers (Champions)	46	24	11	11	1.57	59
2	Darlington	46	25	9	12	1.36	59
3	Torquay United	46	24	10	12	1.47	58
4	Colchester United	46	23	10	13	1.49	56
	Re-elected to Football League						
21	Rochdale	46	16	5	25	0.82	37
22	Lincoln City	46	13	11	22	0.70	37
23	Bradford City	46	12	13	21	0.67	37
24	Wrexham	46	13	9	24	0.69	35

Top goal scorer: Kevin Hector (Bradford Park Avenue) – 44 league goals in the season.

FA Cup Final

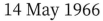

14 May 1966

  Everton 3-2 Sheffield Wednesday

Trebilcock	**McCalliog**
(59, 64 mins)	(4 mins)
Temple	**Ford**
(74 mins)	(57 mins)

Scottish Football League First Division Winners:

Celtic

Scottish Cup Winners:

Rangers

European Cup Winners:

Real Madrid (Spain)

What happened in the United Kingdom in 1966?

Other sport from 1966

 Boxing: Muhammed Ali reigned supreme in heavyweight boxing, including a successful world title defence against the UK's Henry Cooper in March 1966.

 Horse racing: Anglo won the Grand National with jockey Tim Norman on board, while Charlottown, ridden by Scobie Breasley, took the honours in The Derby.

 Athletics: The summer of 1966 saw the Commonwealth Games take place in Kingston, Jamaica. English winners included Mary Rand in the women's long jump and David Hemery in the men's 120 yards hurdles. Jim Alder took gold for Scotland in the men's marathon and the men's long jump was won by Wales' Lynn Davies. Mary Peters of Northern Ireland missed out on a gold medal in the women's shot put by a mere twenty-one centimetres!

 Tennis: Wimbledon's 1966 men's singles winner was Manuel Santana of Spain. It was American Billie Jean King who lifted the ladies' plate for the first of three consecutive titles!

Cricket: West Indies were the summer visitors for this year's test series, racing to a three-one victory over England. West Indian legend, Garry Sobers, averaged a whopping 103 with the bat and took twenty wickets in the series!

 Rugby Union's Five Nations trophy was picked up by Wales, St Helens won the **Rugby League** Championship, the **Formula One** World Drivers' champion was Australia's Jack Brabham, in his Brabham-Repco, and John Pulman of England lifted the World **Snooker** Championship trophy.

News from 1966

 Prime Minister Harold Wilson's Labour Party increased its majority to ninety-six seats on 31 March, having called a snap General Election just a month before.

 The first regular English Channel hovercraft service started in April, carrying passengers from Ramsgate to Calais and back.

 On 6 May, Ian Brady and Myra Hindley were sentenced to life imprisonment for the horrific murders of three children, although there were five victims in total.

 Three plain-clothed police officers were shot dead in August's Shepherd's Bush murders, while investigating a suspicious vehicle.

The Severn Bridge was opened by Her Majesty Queen Elizabeth II on 8 September, connecting the roads of Monmouthshire in south-east Wales to Gloucestershire in west England.

 Buster Edwards returned to face the music in September. He was arrested on his return to London, from Mexico, for his part in 1963's Great Train Robbery.

 The most tragic disaster struck on 21 October when a coal waste tip collapsed in Aberfan, south Wales, killing 116 children and twenty-eight adults. A seventy-six-day tribunal ruled that the National Coal Board was responsible for the disaster.

1966 in film

British Academy for Film and Television Awards (BAFTAs)

 At the 1967 BAFTAs, which celebrates the films of 1966, *The Spy Who Came in from the Cold* swept up many awards. Richard Burton won Best Actor for his portrayal of Alec Leamas, the eponymous spy, pipping Michael Caine as *Alfie* to the gong. Winner of Best Film was *Who's Afraid of Virginia Woolf?* Its star, Elizabeth Taylor, won Best Actress in her lead role as Martha, to make it a husband and wife victory for the top acting awards!

Oscars

Liz Taylor's performance as Martha in *Who's Afraid of Virginia Woolf?* also picked up the Best Actress award at this year's Oscars. But it was period drama, *A Man for All Seasons*, which gathered all the other big awards: Best Actor (Paul Scofield), Best Director (Fred Zinnemann) and Best Picture.

Other notable movie news

Having been released on 29 December 1965, James Bond's *Thunderball*, starring Sean Connery, was a huge success in 1966. It's estimated that the movie took over $140m at the box office worldwide!

1966 in television

It was in January 1966 that *Camberwick Green* first aired as part of the popular *Watch With Mother* series. The animated life at the fictional village remained popular with children for years to come.

William Hartnell became Patrick Troughton in October's *Doctor Who* when the First Doctor 'regenerated' into the Second Doctor.

Coronation Street averaged nearly seventeen million viewers a week in 1966, with notable characters being Ena Sharples (Violet Carson), Len Fairclough (Peter Adamson), Hilda Ogden (Jean Alexander), Jack Walker (Arthur Leslie), Annie Walker (Doris Speed) and mainstay Ken Barlow (William Roach). In May that year, we were introduced to a new resident of Weatherfield. Bet Lynch, played by Julie Goodyear, appeared for nine episodes as a factory worker who was having an affair with the boss, Jack Benjamin. Bet became a fixture on the show from 1970.

 It's estimated nearly a quarter of the UK population watched *The Wednesday Play* when broadcast on 16 November 1966. Ken Loach's *Cathy Come Home* was written by Jeremy Sandford and follows Cathy (Carol White), a young woman who faces a series of unfortunate events that lead her into homelessness and despair.

 On Christmas Day 1966 we might have watched *Aladdin and His Wonderful Lamp* or *The Ken Dodd Show*, or if we fancied a film, *The Comancheros* or *Young At Heart*. This was also the day that the last episode of *Thunderbirds* was broadcast, and we waved goodbye to the 'Supermarionation' Tracy family's International Rescue mission!

1966 in music

Singles

1966's number one slot in the singles' hit parade included
many songs now regarded as classics.

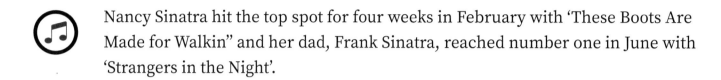

Nancy Sinatra hit the top spot for four weeks in February with 'These Boots Are Made for Walkin'' and her dad, Frank Sinatra, reached number one in June with 'Strangers in the Night'.

From March, The Walker Brothers' hit 'The Sun Ain't Gonna Shine (Anymore)' topped the charts for four weeks.

Dusty Springfield's 'You Don't Have to Say You Love Me' spent a week at number one in April and, the following month, The Rolling Stones had their week at the top with 'Paint it, Black'.

The Beatles had two number ones in '66 with 'Paperback Writer' spending two weeks topping the pops in June, before the double-A-side – 'Yellow Submarine' and 'Eleanor Rigby' – reached number one for four weeks two months later.

The Kinks' 'Sunny Afternoon' had a fortnight topping the charts in July.

In October, Four Tops' 'Reach Out I'll Be There' was number one for three weeks, before being knocked off the top spot by The Beach Boys' classic, 'Good Vibrations'.

But the biggest-selling single of 1966 was Tom Jones' 'Green, Green Grass of Home', which hit the number one spot on 1 December to begin a seven-week run topping the hit parade!

Albums

The LP charts were dominated by one particular record. *The Sound of Music* original soundtrack spent an almost unbelievable thirty-five weeks at number one in 1966, despite having been released in March the previous year! It was number one for a total of twenty weeks the year before and would go on to spend a further fifteen weeks topping the album charts in 1967! Other than the film's main theme, the soundtrack also features 'My Favourite Things', 'Do-Re-Mi' and 'So Long, Farewell'.

The Sound of Music was knocked off the top spot by *Aftermath*, The Rolling Stones LP, which would reach number one for eight weeks from April 1966. The album features the songs 'Mother's Little Helper', 'Under My Thumb' and 'Take it or Leave it', which Mick Jagger and Keith Richards had originally written for The Searchers.

 The only other record to interrupt *The Sound of Music*'s run at the top of the album charts was The Beatles' *Revolver*, which spent seven weeks at number one from August. *Revolver* features 'Eleanor Rigby', 'Yellow Submarine', 'I'm Only Sleeping', 'Good Day Sunshine' and George Harrison's 'Taxman'.

If you subscribe to Spotify, there's a playlist of all the songs mentioned – twenty-three in all – at **bit.ly/4anObuZ** or you can scan the QR code below.

All links are correct at the time of going to print.

Just for fun – it's quiz time!
Answers

1950-1963: A time of disappointment:

a.   Hungarian

1963-1966: The World Cup build-up:

c.   Pickles

11 July 1966: The World Cup kicks off:

a.   World Cup Willie

The group stage:

c.   North Korea

The quarter- and semi-finals:

b.   Eusébio

The final – the first ninety minutes:

b.   Martin Peters

The final – extra time:

c.   Stand up

After the match:

a.   Nobby Stiles

The manager: Sir Alfred 'Alf' Ramsey:

b.   Ipswich Town

Key men from our team and players who didn't play in the final:

a.   Roger Hunt

The one who missed out: James 'Jimmy' Greaves:

a.   AC Milan

The captain: Robert 'Bobby' Moore:

b.   6

The goalkeeper: Gordon Banks:

b.   Mexico, 1970

The virtuoso: Sir Robert 'Bobby' Charlton:

c.   Benfica

The goal machine: Sir Geoffery 'Geoff' Hurst:

a.   Essex

Some more ...
Answers

1.

   a.   Bobby Charlton (England)

2.

   c.   Portugal

3.

   b.   USSR (Soviet Union)

4.

   b.   Eusébio (Portugal)

5.

   a.   Fulham

6.

   c.   49

7.

   a.   Kenneth Wolstenhulme

8.

   a.   Uwe Seeler

9.

   c.   Republic of Ireland

10.

Roker Park – Sunderland
Old Trafford – Manchester United
Hillsborough – Sheffield Wednesday
Ayresome Park – Middlesbrough
Villa Park – Aston Villa
Goodison Park – Everton

Supporters' guide

This section is for the loved ones or carers of people living with dementia or other cognitive difficulties. If you're the carer or a loved one of the person reading this book, you can enjoy it too!

Here are some useful hints and tips to make sure everyone gets the most out of their Cognitive Book.

Scan here for the audio!

1 Follow the instructions to download the free audio at: **cognitivebooks.co.uk/download**

2 The audio really helps support the enjoyment of a Cognitive Book! Encourage the reader – if they are able – to read along while listening.

3

Don't leave this book in amongst other books – like on a bookshelf or in a pile by the bedside.

• •

Always leave the book somewhere it's frequently to hand and easy to access – the armrest of the sofa or a table near where the reader regularly sits, or the bedside table if they like to read at night, for example.

4

For those finding reading more difficult these days, it might be better to stick to the left-hand page of each spread to enjoy the simpler text and vibrant illustrations.

Many readers will be able to explore a Cognitive Book largely on their own – the full text on the right-hand page of each spread will often be accessible to them.

5  **6**

7

Pages 45 to 59 contain exercises you can work on together. Try to support the reader in answering the quiz questions (pages 46-53) and give prompts for the 'Let's chat' questions (page 56).

Cognitive Books are enjoyed by everyone.

They've also been tried and tested on people living with dementia. I didn't start writing Cognitive Books for people with dementia. I wrote for my Dad, Brian. It just so happens he *is* living with dementia. I wanted to create something he'd enjoy today but, equally, something he'd have taken pleasure in reading twenty years ago.

After testing the books with Alzheimer's Society, we realised how many people with and without dementia would enjoy them!
We hope you do too.

Sign up to our mailing list at cognitivebooks.co.uk to discover future titles.

Happy reading!

Matt

Matt Singleton
Author and director of Cognitive Books
cognitivebooks.co.uk

COGNITIVE
BOOKS.